Everybody UP

Student Book 1

Patrick Jackson

Susan Banman Sileci

OXFORD

UNIVERSITY PRESS

OXFORD
UNIVERSITY PRESS

198 Madison Avenue
New York, NY 10016 USA

Great Clarendon Street, Oxford OX2 6DP UK

Oxford University Press is a department of the University of Oxford.
It furthers the University's objective of excellence in research, scholarship,
and education by publishing worldwide in

Oxford   New York

Auckland   Cape Town   Dar es Salaam   Hong Kong   Karachi
Kuala Lumpur   Madrid   Melbourne   Mexico City   Nairobi
New Delhi   Shanghai   Taipei   Toronto

With offices in

Argentina   Austria   Brazil   Chile   Czech Republic   France   Greece
Guatemala   Hungary   Italy   Japan   Poland   Portugal   Singapore
South Korea   Switzerland   Thailand   Turkey   Ukraine   Vietnam

OXFORD and OXFORD ENGLISH are registered trademarks of
Oxford University Press in certain countries.

© Oxford University Press 2012

Database right Oxford University Press (maker)

General Manager, American ELT: Laura Pearson
Executive Publishing Manager: Shelagh Speers
Managing Editor: Clare Hambly
Development Editor: Jennifer Wos
Art, Design, and Production Director: Susan Sanguily
Design Manager: Lisa Donovan
Senior Designer: Molly K. Scanlon
Image Manager: Trisha Masterson
Image Editor: Fran Newman
Production Coordinator: Elizabeth Matsumoto
Senior Manufacturing Controller: Eve Wong

ISBN: 978-0-19-410319-0 Student Book with Audio CD
ISBN: 978-0-19-410320-6 Student Book as pack component
ISBN: 978-0-19-410321-3 Audio CD as pack component

Printed in China

This book is printed on paper from certified and well-managed sources.

10 9 8 7 6 5 4 3 2 1

ACKNOWLEDGMENTS

Oxford University Press would like to thank the thousands of teachers whose
opinions helped to inform this series, and in particular, the following reviewers:

Ayoub Ait Ali, Ministry of Education, Casablanca, Morocco; **Michael P.
Bassett**, Osaka International School, Osaka, Japan; **Paul Richard Batt**, Elephant's
Memory Learning Institute, Taichung; **Jawida Ben Afia**, Inspector General for
Education, Tunis, Tunisia; **Clara Lee Brown**, University of Tennessee, Knoxville,
USA; **Dana Buck**, Margaret Institute of Language (MIL), Chiba, Japan; **Roberta
Calderbank**, Educational Consultant, Riyadh, Saudi Arabia; **Whoisuk Jackie Che**,
Hankuk University of Foreign Studies, Seoul, Korea; **Yuwen Catherine Chen**, Eden
Language Institute, Taichung; **Young-ae Chung**, International Graduate School
of English, Seoul, Korea; **Cláudia Colla de Amorim**, Escola Móbile, São Paulo,
Brazil; **Grace Costa de Oliveira**, Colégio Franciscano Nossa Senhora Aparecida, São
Paulo, Brazil; **Simon Downes**, Kozy Bear School, Tokyo, Japan; **Elaine Elia**, Escola
Caminho Aberto, São Paulo, Brazil; **Mark Evans**, Wisdom BANK Language School,
Kaohsiung; **Sean Gallagher**, Happy English Club, Inc., Nagoya, Japan; **Tania Garcia**,
Montessori Santa Terezinha, São Paulo, Brazil; **Patricia Gazzi**, Cristo Rei School,
São Paulo, Brazil; **Keith Grehan**, Mosaica Education, Abu Dhabi, United Arab
Emirates; **Anna Kyungmi Han**, EB (English Break) Language School, Paju, Korea;
Briony Hewitt, ILA Vietnam, Ho Chi Minh City, Vietnam; **Kelly Hsu**, Kelly English
School, Tainan; **Kyla KCW Huang**, Kang Ning English School, Hsinchu; **Lilian
Itzicovitch Leventhal**, Colegio I.L. Peretz, São Paulo, Brazil; **Aaron Jolly**, Hanseo
University, Seosan, Korea; **Sean Pan-Seob Kim**, Kangseo Wonderland, Seoul, Korea;
Charlotte Lee, Jordan's Language School Headquarters, Taipei; **Hsiang-pao Sarah
Lin**, Lincoln International Language School, Tainan; **David Martin**, Busy Beavers
English Resources, Vancouver, Canada; **Conrad Matsumoto**, Conrad's English House,
Odawara, Japan; **Daniel McNeill**, Yokohama YMCA, Yokohama, Japan; **Sung Hee
Park**, Yonsei University Graduate School of Education, Anyang, Korea; **Juliana
Queiroz Pereira**, Colégio Marista Arquidiocesano and Colégio I. L. Peretz, São
Paulo, Brazil; **Sandra Puccioni Katsuda**, Colégio Montessori Santa Terezinha, São
Paulo, Brazil; **Saba'a Qhadi**, University of Qatar, Doha, Qatar; **Karyna Ribeiro**,
Colégio Miguel de Cervantes, São Paulo, Brazil; **Charlie Richards**, The Learning
Tree English School, Osaka, Japan; **Mark Riley**, Shane English School, Taipei;
John Sanders, Camelot English Study Centre, Tokyo, Japan; **Kaj Schwermer**,
Eureka Learning Institute, Osaka, Japan; **Monika Soens Yang**, Taipei European
School, Taipei; **Jiyeon Song**, Seoul, Korea; **Jason Stewart**, Taejeon International
Language School, Daejeon, Korea; **David Stucker**, Myojo Elementary School, Beppu,
Japan; **Andrew Townshend**, Natural English School, Tokyo, Japan; **Thanaphong
Udomsab**, Petchaburi Rajabhat University, Petchaburi, Thailand; **Aliéte Mara
Ventura**, Escola Carandá, São Paulo, Brazil; **Ariel Yao**, Ren Da English School,
Taipei.

Cover Design: Molly K. Scanlon

Illustrations by: Charlene Chua: 2, 4, 6, 8, 9 (top), 12, 14 (bottom), 16, 17 (top), 22,
24 (bottom), 26, 27 (top), 30, 31 (top), 32 (bottom), 34, 35 (top), 40, 42 (bottom), 44,
45 (top), 48, 50, 52, 53 (top), 58 (bottom), 60 (bottom), 62, 63 (top), 66 (bottom), 68
(bottom), 70, 71(top), Andy Elkerton: 9 (border, bottom), 24 (top), 25, 42 (top), 43,
51, 58 (top), 59, 60 (top), 61, 71 (border, bottom); Ken Gamage: 7, 13, 15, 28, 29, 32
(top), 33 (border, spot art), 66 (top), 67 (mid., bottom); Anna Godwin: 41, 46, 47, 55;
Jannie Ho: 5, 23, 35 (border, bottom), 38, 39, 49, 64 (bottom), 65, 74, 75; Nathan
Jarvis: 3, 14 (top), 17 (border, bottom), 20, 21, 27 (border, bottom), 33 (boy), 45
(border, bottom), 53 (border, bottom), 56, 57, 63 (border, bottom), 64 (top), 67 (top),
68 (top), 69; John Kurtz: (kid style art) 5, 7, 13, 25, 31, 36, 49, 73; Schuster: 72.

Commissioned photography by: Richard Hutchings/Digital Light Source, Cover photos
and all photos of kids in lower right hand corner of pages: 2, 5, 7, 9, 11, 13, 15, 17,
19, 23, 25, 27, 29, 31, 33, 35, 37, 41, 43, 45, 47, 49, 51, 53, 55, 59, 61, 63, 65, 67,
69, 71, and 73. Haddon Davies, 30 (mother); 30 (brother); Dennis Kitchen Studio,
Inc., 4 (pencil); 5 (pencil); 5 (backpack); Mark Mason, 6 (notebook); 19 (banana); and
Michael Steinhofer, 46–47 (forest background).

*The publishers would like to thank the following for their kind permission to reproduce
photographs:* Galushko Sergey/Shutterstock, 4 (pen); Podfoto/Shutterstock, 4
(backpack); magicoven/Shutterstock, 4 (eraser); Stockbyte, 4 (ruler); Rafael
Fernandez Torres/Shutterstock, 4 (pencil case); Galushko Sergey/Shutterstock, 5
(pen); Peter Guess/Shutterstock, 5 (ruler); Paul Matthew Photography/Shutterstock,
5 (eraser); Andy Crawford, 5 (pencil case); cloki/Shutterstock, 6 (textbook); Corbis,
6 (desk); Zedcor Wholly Owned, 6 (chair); Stockbyte, 11 (ruler); Fanfo/Shutterstock,
11 (pizza); C Squared Studios, 11 (book); Photodisc, 11 (bread); ©2008 Jupiter
Images, 11 (notebook); Yuri Shirokov/Shutterstock, 12(paint); Stephen Aaron Rees/
Shutterstock, 12 (color paper); UltraOrto, S.A./Shutterstock, 12 (chalk); Denis and
Yulia Pogostins/Shutterstock, 12 (yarn); Photodisc, 12 (glue); Sean Nel/Shutterstock,
12 (tape); J.D.S./Shutterstock, 18–19 (background splotches); SunLu4ik/Shutterstock,
18 (watercolor paints); Edyta Pawlowska/Shutterstock, 18 (paint palette/brush); Yuri
Shirokov/Shutterstock, 18 (paint); Photodisc, 19 (grass); Aaron Amat/Shutterstock.
com, 19 (jelly); ultimathule/Shutterstock, 19 (fabric); mitzy/Shutterstock, 19
(orange rind); Photodisc, 19 (blueberries); cardiae/Shutterstock, 19 (cotton ball);
steamroller_blues/Shutterstock, 19 (fur); Eky Chan/Shutterstock, 19 (leaf); Digital
Vision, 19 (elephant skin); Photodisc, 19 (flower petals); Shane White/Shutterstock,
28 (abacus); Stockbyte, 30 (father); Nathan Blaney, 30 (sister); Photodisc, 30
(grandmother); Photodisc, 30 (grandfather); Moodboard, 31 (father and mother);
Comstock Images, 31 (sister); Photodisc, 31 (grandmother and grandfather);
Digital Vision, 31 (brother); Photodisc, 36 (rice bowl); luchschen/Shutterstock, 36
(pizza); D. Hurst, 36 (cake); Ingram, 36 (bread); Unarmed/Shutterstock, 41 (bread);
Digital Vision, 41 (tree); Laura Ciapponi, 41 (lake); Photodisc, 4 (river); DEA/M.
SANTINI/De Agostini/Getty Images, 41 (rock); Vincenzo Lombardo, 41 (hill); Sabine
Scheckel, 46–47 (twig frame); Ingram, 46 (turtle); Cynthia Kidwell/Shutterstock, 46
(frog); Dawid Zagorski/Shutterstock, 46 (spider); Evgeniy Ayupov/Shutterstock, 46
(ant); maxstockphoto /Shutterstock, 46 (leaf); Photodisc, 46 (monkey); Photodisc,
48 (elephant); Photodisc, 48 (tiger); John E Marriott, 48 (bear); Photodisc, 48
(kangaroo); Ingram, 48 (penguin); Photodisc, 50 (snake); Ingram, 50 (giraffe);
Photodisc, 50 (lion); Ingram, 50 (zebra); Corbis/Digital Stock, 50 (zebras); Corel,
54 (kangaroo hopping); Photodisc, 5 (bears swimming); Photodisc, 54 (elephants
walking); Photodisc, 54 (zebras); Photodisc, 54 (penguins); Corbis, 54 (bears); Corel,
54 (kangaroos); ©PhotoSpin, Inc/Alamy, 54 (snake); Kitch Bain/Shutterstock, 54
(elephants section B.); Reed/Shutterstock, 55 (binoculars); ©Lawrence Manning/
Corbis, 64 (toothpaste); Ingram, 64 (toothbrush); shcherbina galyna/Shutterstock,
64 (soap background); rchana bharti/Shutterstock, 72 (train); Vibrant Image Studio/
Shutterstock, 72 (school bus); Ken Davies/Masterfile, 72 (truck); JEO/Shutterstock,
72 (tugboat).

Music by:
Julie Gold: 3, 15, 17, 51, 53
Red Grammer: 9, 33, 43, 45
Troy McDonald and Devon Thagard: 25, 27, 61, 63
Ilene Weiss: 7, 35, 69, 71

For darling Ami. Thank you for all the help with Daddy's homework.
—P.J.

For my incredible family—Riccardo, Audrey, and Natalie.
—S.B.S.

Table of Contents

Welcome

A Listen, point, and say. CD1 03

1. Hi. I'm Danny.

2. Hello. My name is Emma.

3. Hello. I'm Julie.

4. Hi. My name is Mike.

Danny   **Emma**   **Julie**   **Mike**

B Listen, ask, and answer. Then practice. CD1 04

| What's your name? | I'm / My name is | Danny. |

What's = What is
I'm = I am

Hi. What's your name?

C Sing. CD1 05 »)

The Alphabet

Aa Bb Cc Dd Ee Ff Gg Hh
Ii Jj Kk Ll Mm Nn Oo Pp Qq
Rr Ss Tt Uu Vv Ww Xx Yy Zz

03

D Listen, point, and say. CD1 06 »)

1.

Listen.

2.

Point.

3.

Count.

4.

Talk.

5.

Ask.

6.

Answer.

04

1 First Day

A Listen, point, and say. CD1 07

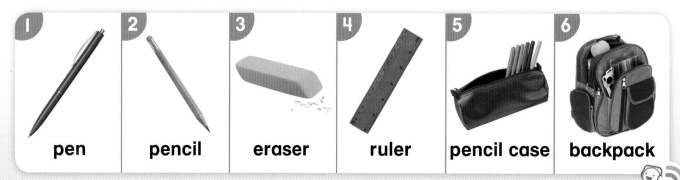

1	2	3	4	5	6
pen	pencil	eraser	ruler	pencil case	backpack

05

B Listen and find. CD1 08

C Listen and say. Then practice. CD1 09•))

It's | a pen.
an eraser.

It's = It is

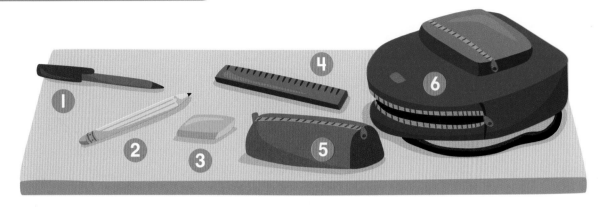

D Listen, ask, and answer. Then practice. CD1 10•))

What is it?
It's a pen.

It's = It is

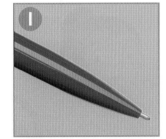
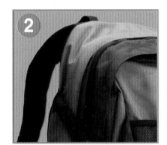

E Look at B. Point, ask, and answer.

What is it?

It's a ruler.

What is it?

A **Listen, point, and say.** CD1 11

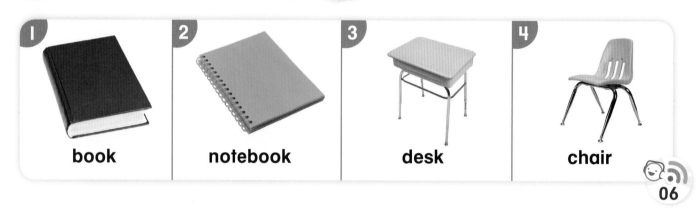

1	2	3	4
book	notebook	desk	chair

06

B **Listen and say. Then practice.** CD1 12

It's a book. It isn't a notebook.

It's = It is
isn't = is not

3 Julie

4

Danny

Mike

1

Emma

2

C Sing.

It's a Book

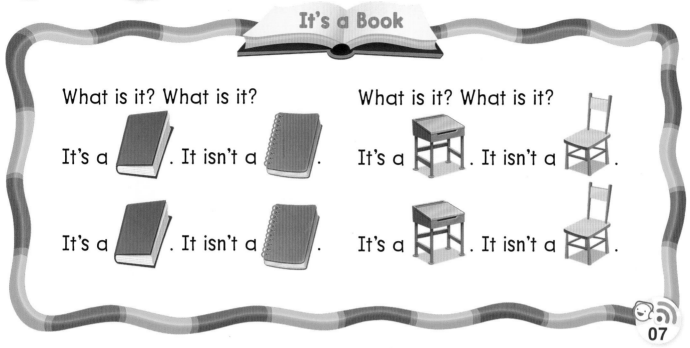

What is it? What is it?

It's a ___. It isn't a ___.

It's a ___. It isn't a ___.

What is it? What is it?

It's a ___. It isn't a ___.

It's a ___. It isn't a ___.

07

D Listen and number. CD1 14

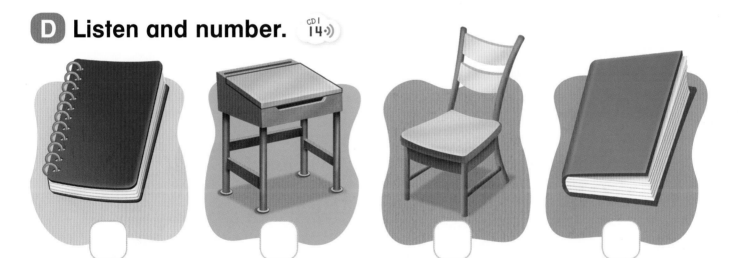

E Look around your classroom. Point and say.

It's a desk.

It isn't a chair.

It's a chair.

A **Talk about the pictures. Then listen and read.**

I'm Great!

B Listen and number.

C Sing.

Hi! How are You?

Hi! How are you?

  I'm fine. Thank you.

How are you?

I'm fine. Thank you!

How are you?

  I'm fine! How are you?

I'm OK! How are you?

  I'm fine. I'm great!

08

D Listen and say. Then act.

How are you?

I'm fine. Thank you.

I'm great. How are you?

Math

A Listen, point, and say. CD1 19

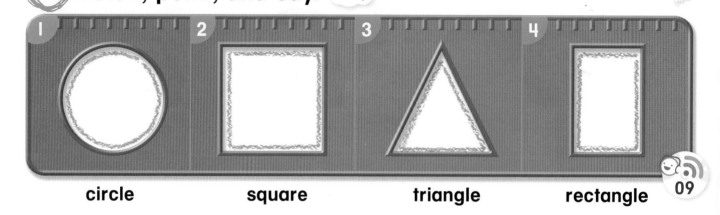

1	2	3	4
circle	square	triangle	rectangle

09

B Listen, ask, and answer. Then practice. CD1 20

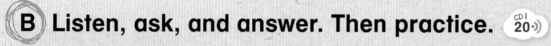

Is it a circle?   Yes, it is.
No, it isn't.

isn't = is not

1.

2.

3.

4.

C Match.

1. 2. 3. 4. 5.

D Look at C. Ask and answer.

Is it a triangle?

Yes, it is.

Look! It's a rectangle.

E Look around your classroom. Find shapes.

Look! It's a square.

Look! It's a circle.

2 Art Class

Lesson 1 Art Supplies

A Listen, point, and say. CD1 21

1	2	3	4	5	6

paint	paper	chalk	yarn	glue	tape

B Listen and find. CD1 22

C Listen and say. Then practice. CD1 23

This is paint.

1.    2.   3.    4.   5.   6.

D Listen, ask, and answer. Then practice. CD1 24

What's this?
This is paint.

What's = What is

E Look at **B**. Point, ask, and answer.

What's this?

This is yarn.

What's this?

Lesson 2 Colors

A Listen, point, and say. CD1 25

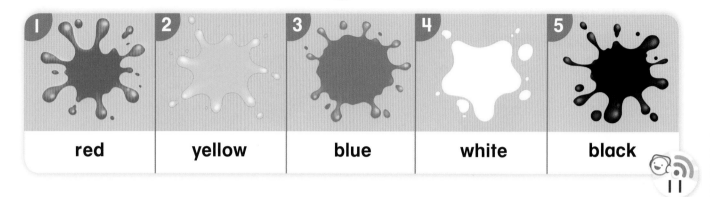

1	2	3	4	5
red	yellow	blue	white	black

B Listen, ask, and answer. Then practice. CD1 26

What color is it?
It's red.

It's = It is

C Sing.

Colors!

Red. Yellow. Blue. White. Black.

What color is it?

It's ____. It's ____. It's ____.

What color is it?

It's ____. It's ____, ____, ____.

12

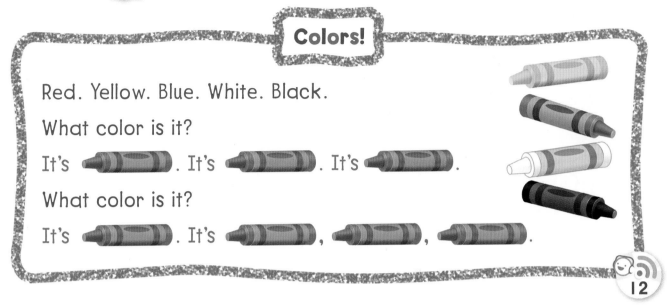

D Listen and circle.

1. a / b
2. a / b
3. a / b
4. a / b
5. a / b

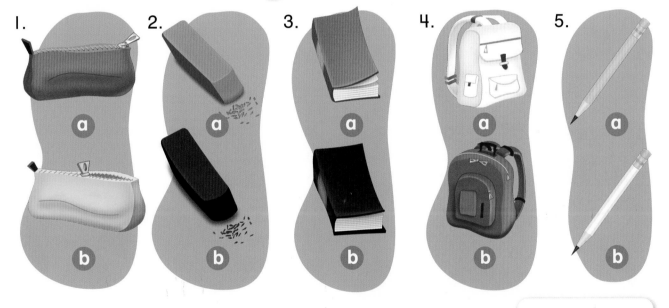

My pencil is red.

E Look around your classroom. Point, ask, and answer.

What's this?

It's a backpack. It's blue.

A Talk about the pictures. Then listen and read.

The Blue Paint

B Listen and number. CD1 30

Blue

Red
Yellow

Blue

White
Black

C Sing. CD1 31

Let's Share

This is my paint. This is my paint.

Hey! It's my paint, too!

OK. Let's share. Let's share. Let's share.

OK. Let's share. Let's share. OK. Cool.

13

D Listen and say. Then act. CD1 32

Let's share.

OK.

2

3

It's red!

Lesson 4 Colors

Art

A Listen, point, and say. CD1 33

1	2	3	4	5	6
green	purple	orange	pink	gray	brown

14

B Listen and say. Then practice. CD1 34

Blue **and** yellow **make** green.

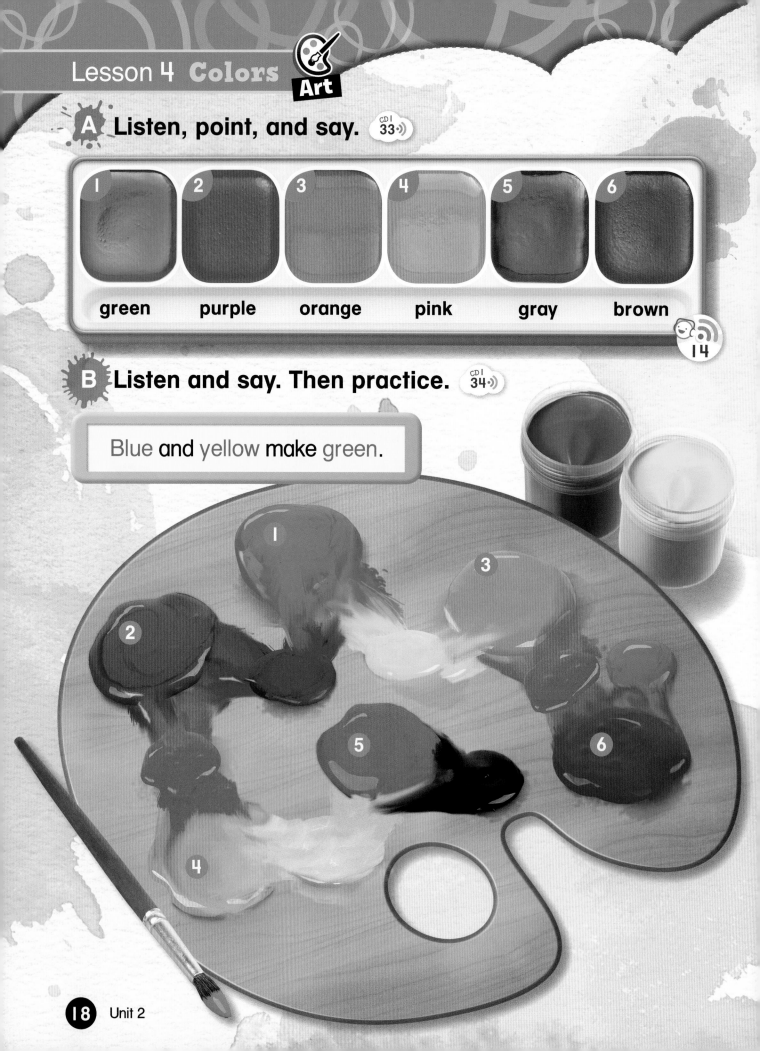

C What color is it? Ask and answer.

 1

 2

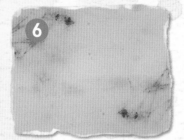 3

 4

 5

 6

 7

 8

9

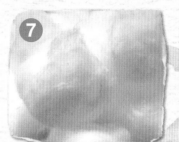 10

 11

 10

D Look around your classroom. Find and say the colors.

Look! It's red.

Look! It's purple.

My backpack is green. Blue and yellow make green.

red	✓	purple	
orange		pink	
yellow		white	
green		black	
blue		gray	
brown			

Review 1

A I can say these words.

1.
2.
3.
4.
5.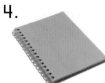
6.

7.
8.
9.
10.
11.
12.

B I can talk about these topics.

1.
2.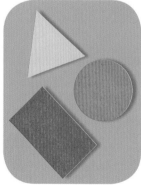
3.
4.

school supplies   shapes   art supplies   colors

C I can talk with you.

1.

How are you?

2.

OK.

A Listen, point, and say. (CD1 35)

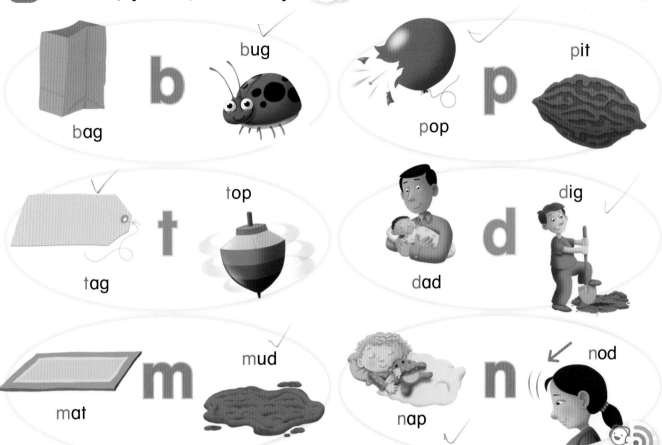

bug

b

bag

pit

p

pop

top

t

tag

dig

d

dad

mud

m

mat

nod

n

nap

15

B Look at A. Point and say with a partner.

C Listen and circle. (CD1 36)

1.

   d   t

2.

   m   n

3.

   b   p

4.

   n   m

5.

   p   b

6.

   t   d

3 Birthday Party

A Listen, point, and say. CD1 37

1	2	3	4	5	6
one	two	three	four	five	six
7	8	9	10	11	12
seven	eight	nine	ten	eleven	twelve

16

B Listen and find. CD1 38

Happy Birthday!

C Listen and say. Then practice. 🔊 CD1 39

I'm seven.   I'm = I am

D Listen, ask, and answer. Then practice. 🔊 CD1 40

How old are you?
I'm eight.   I'm = I am

1.

2.

3.

4.

5.

6.

E Look at B. Say the numbers.

4, 8, 1...

6, 5, 7...

I'm eight.
How old are you?

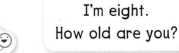

A Listen, point, and say.

1  doll	2  ball

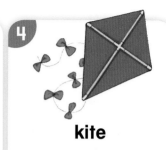 car

4 kite

dolls

balls

cars

kites

B Listen, ask, and answer. Then practice.

How many dolls?　　One doll.
　　　　　　　　　　Two dolls.

Toys

Happy Birthday!

How Many Dolls?

How many dolls?　One for you,

One doll.　And one for me.

How many dolls?　How many dolls?

Two dolls.　Two dolls.

18

D Make a number book. Show and tell.

One kite. Six kites.

1　6

Look!
How many balls?

E Look at your number books.
Ask and answer.

How many kites?

Six kites.

A Talk about the pictures. Then listen and read.

My Turn!

B Listen and number.

C Sing.

Let's Play Together

It's your turn.

    Let's play together.

It's my turn.

    Let's play together.

It's your turn.

    Thank you.

It's my turn.

    Good job!

19

D Listen and say. Then act.

It's your turn.

Thank you.

It's my birthday!

1

2

3

A Listen, point, and say.

1. game
2. marble
3. puzzle
4. card

B Listen and say. Then practice.

I have | one game.
two games.

games   marbles
puzzles cards

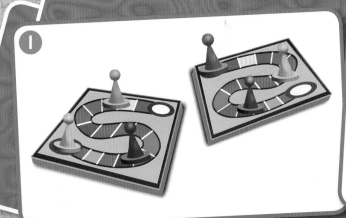

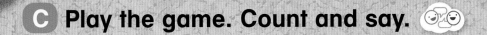

C Play the game. Count and say.

I have two kites.

I have six cards.

I have four puzzles.

D What about you?

I have seven cards.

I have twelve marbles.

4 Home

A Listen, point, and say. CD1 50

1	2	3	4	5	6

mother	father	brother	sister	grandmother	grandfather

B Listen and find. CD1 51

C Listen and say. Then practice. CD1 52

This is my mother.

D Listen, ask, and answer. Then practice. CD1 53

Who's this?
This is my mother.

Who's = Who is

E Look at B. Point, ask, and answer.

Who's this?

This is my brother.

This is my sister.

My Family

A **Listen, point, and say.** CD1 54

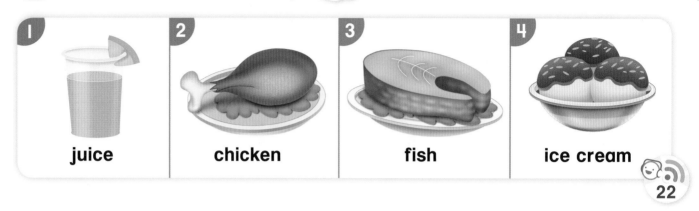

1	2	3	4
juice	chicken	fish	ice cream

22

B **Listen and say. Then practice.** CD1 55

I	like don't like	juice.

don't = do not

C Sing. CD1 56

I Like Chicken!

I like 🍗. I like 🐟. I like 🍚.
What's this? This is 🧃.
Uh, oh! Uh, oh! I don't like 🧃!
🍗, 🍗, 🍚, 🐟. I like 🍚.
What's this? This is 🧃. This is 🧃.
Uh, oh! Uh, oh! Uh, oh!

23

D What about you? Draw 😊 or 😝.

		I like	I don't like
1. ice cream			
2. juice			
3. fish			
4. chicken			

I like chicken. What about you?

E Look at D. Talk with your partner.

I like ice cream.

I don't like chicken.

A Talk about the pictures. Then listen and read.

B Listen and number.

C Sing.

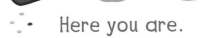

Thank You!

Here you are.

A cookie? For me?

Yes, for you. A cookie!

Here you are.

Thank you! Thank you! Thank you!

You're welcome.

24

D Listen and say. Then act.

Here you are. Thank you.

You're welcome.

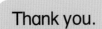

I like cookies, too!

Lesson 3 **35**

A **Listen, point, and say.** CD1 61

1 pizza

2 rice

3 cake

4 bread

25

B **Listen, ask, and answer. Then practice.** CD1 62

What's this?
  This is pizza. I like pizza.

What's = What is

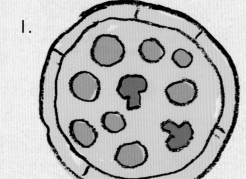

1.

2.

3.

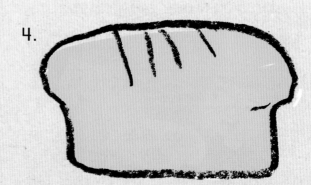

4.

C **Draw food pictures.**

I like

I don't like

D **Look at your food pictures. Ask and answer.**

I like ice cream.
I don't like fish.

What's this?

This is cake.
I like cake.

Review 2

A I can say these words.

1.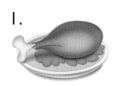
2.
3.
4.
5.
6.

7.
8.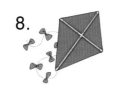
9.
10.
11.
12.

B I can talk about these topics.

1.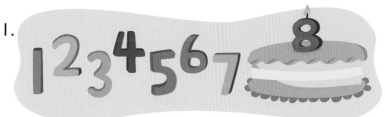

numbers

2.

toys

3.

family

4.

food

C I can talk with you.

1.

Thank you.

2.

You're welcome.

A Listen, point, and say. CD1 63

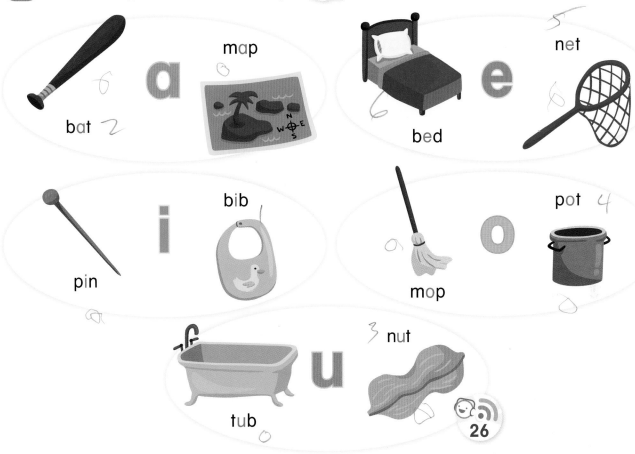

bat   **a**   map

bed   **e**   net

pin   **i**   bib

mop   **o**   pot

tub   **u**   nut

26

B Look at **A**. Point and say with a partner.

C Listen and circle. CD1 64

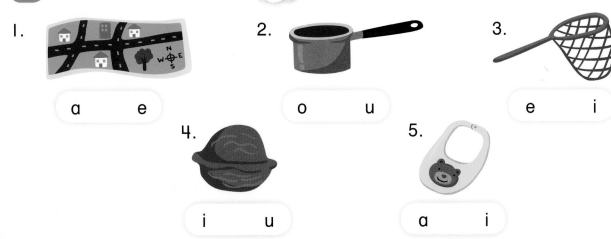

1.   a   e

2.   o   u

3.   e   i

4.   i   u

5.   a   i

5 The Park

Lesson 1 Nature

A Listen, point, and say. CD2 02

1	2	3	4	5	6
flower	tree	rock	river	hill	lake

27

B Listen and find. CD2 03

C Listen and say. Then practice. CD2 04))

I can see | a flower.
flowers.

flowers   trees
rocks   rivers
hills   lakes

1.  2.  3.  4.  5.  6.

D Listen, ask, and answer. Then practice. CD2 05))

What can you see?   I can see | a flower.
flowers.

E Look at B. Point, ask, and answer.

What can you see?

I can see trees.

I can see trees.

Lesson 2 Playtime

A Listen, point, and say. CD2 06

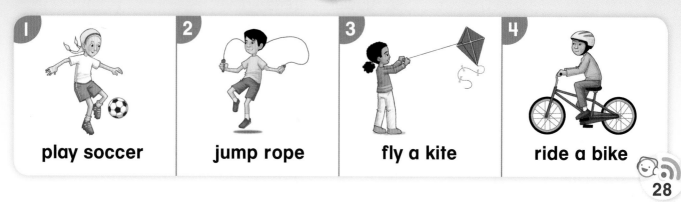

1	2	3	4
play soccer	jump rope	fly a kite	ride a bike

28

B Listen and say. Then practice. CD2 07

I	can can't	play soccer.

can't = can not

C Sing.

I Can!

I can! I can't! I can! I can't!   I can't! I can! I can't! I can!

I can 🏀. I can't 🪁.   I can't ⚽. I can 🪁.

I can 〰️. I can't 🚲.   I can't 〰️. I can 🚲.

I can see a ball, ✸ and ⬤.   I can't see a ball, ✸ and ⬤.

What about you?   I can see you!

29

D What about you?

	I can	I can't
1. play soccer ⚽		
2. ride a bike 🚲		
3. jump rope 〰️		
4. fly a kite 🪁		

I can jump rope!

E Look at D. Talk with your partner.

I can play soccer.

I can't fly a kite.

A **Talk about the pictures. Then listen and read.**

My Kite!

Oh, no! My kite!

Sure.

Dad, please help me!

OK! Thanks, Dad.

You're welcome.

Oops!

I can help you, Dad.

Be helpful.

B Listen and number. CD2 10

C Sing. CD2 11

Help Me!

Help me! Help me! Help me, Dad.
I can't ride a bike.
Help me! Help me! Help me, Dad.
　I can help you, Mike!
　I can help you
　　ride a bike.

Thank you, Dad.
　You're welcome, Mike.
Help me! Help me!
　I can help you.
Thank you, Dad.
　You're welcome, Mike.

30

D Listen and say. Then act. CD2 12

I can help!

Please help me.

Sure.

1

2

3

Lesson 3   45

A Listen, point, and say.

1  turtle	**2**  frog	**3**  spider	**4** 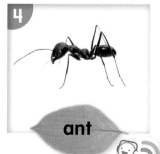 ant

B Listen, ask, and answer. Then practice.

Can you see | a turtle? Yes, I can.
an ant? No, I can't.

can't = can not

1 	**2** 	**3** 	**4** 
5 	**6** 	**7** 	**8** 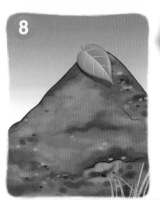

C What can you see? Circle and count.

How many?

	How many?
turtle	4
frog	
spider	
mountain	
tree	
rock	
leaf	
bird	
path	
ant	

D Look at C. Ask and answer.

What can you see?

I can see three spiders.

Can you see a tree?

6 The Zoo

A Listen, point, and say. CD2 15

1	2	3	4	5	6

monkey	elephant	tiger	bear	kangaroo	penguin

32

B Listen and find. CD2 16

C Listen and say. Then practice.

The monkey is in the tree.

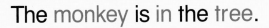

in   on   under

1.

2.

3.

4.

5.

6.

D Listen, ask, and answer. Then practice.

Where is the monkey?
It's on the rock.

It's = It is

5

1 2 3 4 6

E Look at B. Point, ask, and answer.

Where is the penguin?

It's in the lake.

The elephant
is on the rock.

A **Listen, point, and say.** CD2 19

1	2	3	4
snake	giraffe	lion	zebra

33

B **Listen, ask, and answer. Then practice.** CD2 20

> Where are the snakes?
> They're on the rock.

They're = They are

snakes
giraffes
lions
zebras

C Sing.

CD2 21

Where Is the Snake?

Where is the snake?

It's under the rock.

The rock is under the tree.

Zebras, giraffes, lions, and bears

Look up at the monkey.

The monkey is in the tree.

34

D Make a zoo book. Show and tell.

The elephant is under the tree.
The monkeys are in the tree.

E Look at your zoo books.
Ask and answer.

Where are the monkeys?

Where is the elephant?

It's under the tree.

A Talk about the pictures. Then listen and read.

B Listen and number. CD2 23))

C Sing. CD2 24))

Hurry!

Hurry, hurry, hurry, hurry!
Oh, no! I'm sorry.
Hurry, hurry, hurry!
I'm sorry.
That's OK.

Oops! Uh, oh!
Yikes! Oh, no!
I'm sorry.
That's OK.

35

D Listen and say. Then act. CD2 25))

I like bears!

I'm sorry.

That's OK.

Science

A **Listen, point, and say.** CD2 26

1 **run**

2 **hop**

3 **swim**

4 **walk**

36

B **Listen, ask, and answer. Then practice.** CD2 27

| Can | zebras penguins | run? | Yes, they can. No, they can't. |

can't = can not

1 **zebras**
run ✓
hop ✗
swim ✓
walk ✓

2 **elephants**
run ✓
hop ✗
swim ✓
walk ✓

3 **penguins**
run ✗
hop ✓
swim ✓
walk ✓

4 **bears**
run ✓
hop ✗
swim ✓
walk ✓

5 **kangaroos**
run ✗
hop ✓
swim ✓
walk ✗

6 **snakes**
run ✗
hop ✗
swim ✓
walk ✗

1.

walk	run
(swim)	hop

2.

walk	run
swim	hop

3.

walk	run
swim	hop

4.

walk	run
swim	hop

5.

walk	run
swim	hop

6.

walk	run
swim	hop

D **Look at** **C** .
Ask and answer.

I can hop!

Can penguins run?

No, they can't.

Review 3

A I can say these words.

1.
2.
3.
4.
5.
6.

7.
8.
9.
10.
11.
12.

B I can talk about these topics.

1.
2.
3.
4.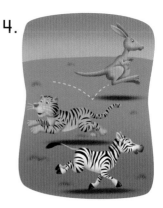

nature   playtime   animals   abilities

C I can talk with you.

1.

Sure.

2.

I'm sorry.

A Listen, point, and say. CD2 29

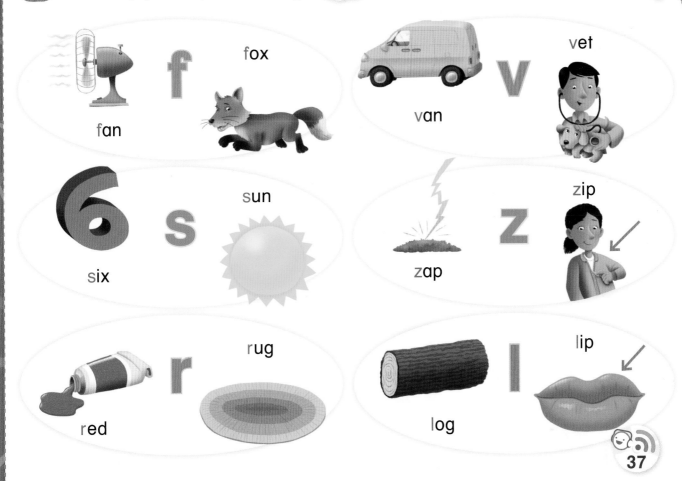

fan **f** fox

van **V** vet

six **s** sun

zap **Z** zip

red **r** rug

log **l** lip

37

B Look at Ⓐ. Point and say with a partner.

C Listen and circle. CD2 30

1.

r   l

2.

f   v

3.

s   z

4.

l   r

5.

v   f

6.

z   s

7 Science Day

A Listen, point, and say. CD2 31

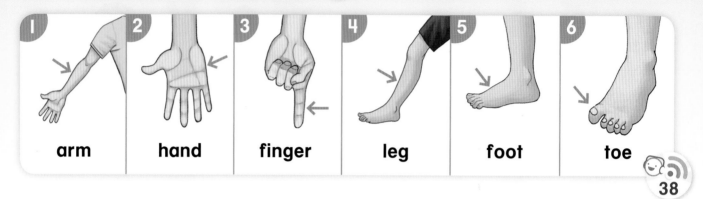

1	2	3	4	5	6
arm	hand	finger	leg	foot	toe

38

B Listen and find. CD2 32

Welcome to the Science Museum

C **Listen, ask, and answer. Then practice.** CD2 33

What's this?
This is my arm.

What's = What is

D **Listen, ask, and answer. Then practice.** CD2 34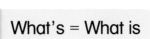

What are these?
These are my arms.

arms	hands	fingers
legs	feet	toes

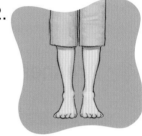

1.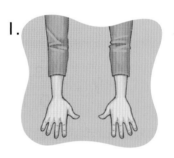

2.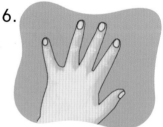

3.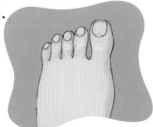

4.

5.

6.

E **Look at B. Point, ask, and answer.**

What are these?

These are my legs.

These are my hands.

A Listen, point, and say. CD2 35

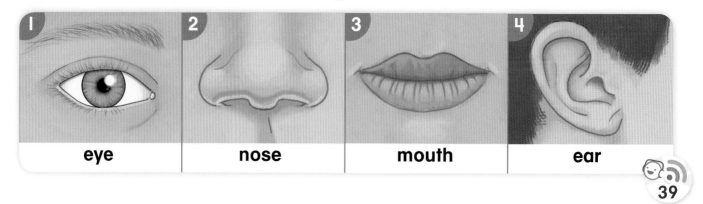

| 1 | 2 | 3 | 4 |
| eye | nose | mouth | ear |

39

B Listen, ask, and answer. Then practice. CD2 36

| Is this my eye? | Yes, it is.
No, it isn't. |
| Are these my eyes? | Yes, they are.
No, they aren't. |

isn't = is not
aren't = are not

eyes   ears

1.

2.

3.

4.

5.

6.

C Sing. CD2 37

This Is Me

This is my 🖐. This is my 🖐.
These are my 🖐🖐.
This is my 🦶. This is my 🦶.
These are my 🦶🦶.
Clap. Clap. Stomp. Stomp.

This is my 👁. This is my 👁.
These are my 👁 👁.
This is my 👂. This is my 👂.
These are my 👂 👂.
Look. Look. Listen. Listen.

40

D Trace your partner.

Are these my ears?

E Look at your drawing. Ask and answer.

Are these my legs?

Yes, they are.

A Talk about the pictures. Then listen and read.

I Can't See!

B Listen and number. (CD2 39)

C Sing. (CD2 40)

Excuse Me

Excuse me. Excuse me.

I can't see.

Excuse me. Excuse me.

I can't see.

Tap, tap, tap. Excuse me!

Tap, tap, tap. Excuse me!

41

D Listen and say. Then act. (CD2 41)

Look! I can jump.

Excuse me.

Sure.

Thank you.

2

3

Lesson 4 Healthy Habits

 Health

A Listen, point, and say. CD2 42

1	2	3	4
wash my face	wash my hands	brush my hair	brush my teeth

42

B Listen and say. Then practice. CD2 43

I can wash my face.

1

2

3

4

C Look and write.

eye   mouth
ear   foot
arm   toe
leg   finger
hand   nose

eye

D Talk with your classmates.

I have two eyes.

I have ten fingers.

I can wash my hands.

8 The Toy Store

Lesson 1 Adjectives

A Listen, point, and say. CD2 44

1. old
2. new
3. big
4. small
5. long
6. short

43

B Listen and find. CD2 45

C Listen and say. Then practice. CD2 46

That's an old bike.
Those are new bikes.

That's = That is

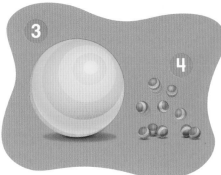

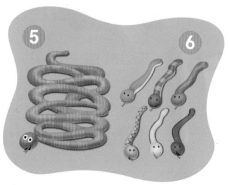

1 2 3 4 5 6

D Listen, ask, and answer. Then practice. CD2 47

What's that?	What are those?
That's an old doll.	Those are new bikes.

What's = What is
That's = That is

1 2 3 4 5 6

This is my new ball!

E Look at **B**. Point, ask, and answer.

What's that?

That's an old bear.

A Listen, point, and say. CD2 48

1	2	3	4
fast	slow	noisy	quiet

44

B Listen, ask, and answer. Then practice. CD2 49

Is that a fast car?
Yes, it is.
No, it isn't.

isn't = is not
aren't = are not

Are those fast cars?
Yes, they are.
No, they aren't.

Start

RRR...

RRR...

Finish

C Sing.  CD2 50

Fast Cars!

Is that a fast car?
  Yes, it is. Yes, it is. Yes, it is.
Is that a fast car?
  Yes, it is.
  That is a fast car.

Are those slow cars?
  No, they aren't.
Are those fast cars?
  Yes, they are!
  Yes, they are!

noisy
quiet

45

D Make a car book. Show and tell.

That's a fast car.

a fast car

a slow car

I'm fast!

E Look at your car books. Ask and answer.

Is that a fast car?

Yes, it is.

A **Talk about the pictures. Then listen and read.**

B Listen and number. (CD2 52)

C Sing. (CD2 53)

Please Be Quiet

Please be quiet! Please be quiet! Please be quiet!

Please be quiet! Please be quiet! Please be quiet!

Please be quiet!

Please be quiet.

OK. I'm sorry.

Thanks.

46

D Listen and say. Then act. (CD2 54)

Please be quiet.

OK. I'm sorry.

Thanks.

Please be quiet.

Lesson 3 **71**

Lesson 4 Transportation

Social Studies

A Listen, point, and say. CD2 55

1	2	3	4
bus	truck	train	boat

47

B Listen, ask, and answer. Then practice. CD2 56

What's	this? that?	It's an old bus.
What are	these? those?	They're new buses.

What's = What is
It's = It is
They're = They are

buses   trucks
trains   boats

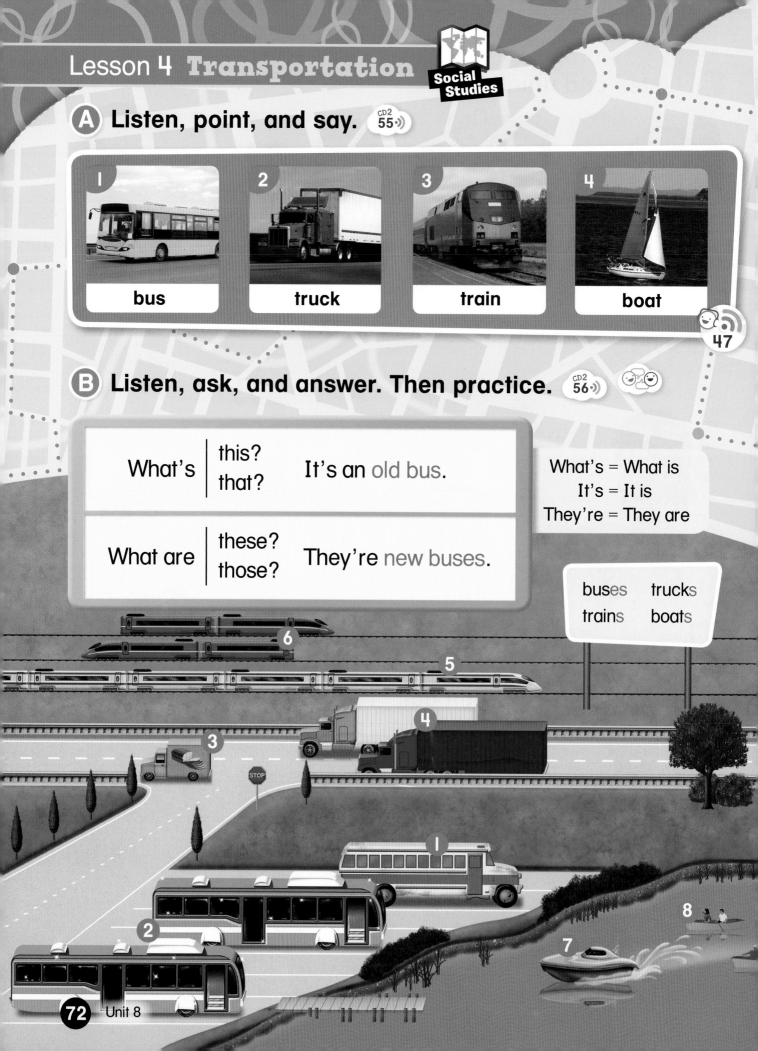

C Listen. Fill in the chart. CD2 57

	this	that	these	those
1. bus			✓	
2. train				
3. boat				
4. truck				
5. car				
6. bike				

My bike is fast!

D Look at **B**.
Talk with your partner.

What's this?

It's a fast boat.

Lesson 4 73

Review 4

A I can say these words.

1.
2.
3.
4.
5.
6.

7.
8.
9.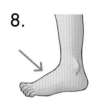
10.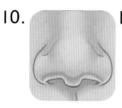
11.
12.

B I can talk about these topics.

1.
my body

2.
my face

3.
healthy habits

4.
adjectives

5.
adjectives

6.
transportation

C I can talk with you.

1.

Sure.

2.

Thanks.

Phonics

Bonus

A Listen, point, and say. CD2 58

vase

a_e

rake

peek

ee

beet

lime

i_e

dive

bone

o_e

rose

mule

u_e

cube 48

B Look at A. Point and say with a partner.

C Listen and circle. CD2 59

1.

  o   u

2.   a   i

3.

  u   o

4.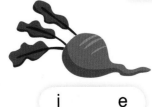

  i   e

5.

  i   a

Phonics 4 **75**

Syllabus

Welcome

Hi.
Hello.

What's your name?
I'm Danny.
My name is Danny.

Classroom Verbs:
listen   point
count   talk
ask   answer

Unit 1 First Day

Lesson 1	Lesson 2	Lesson 3	Lesson 4
School Supplies: pen, pencil, eraser, ruler, pencil case, backpack	**School Supplies:** book, notebook, desk, chair	**Story: I'm Great!**	**Shapes:** circle, square, triangle, rectangle
It's a pen. It's an eraser. What is it? It's a pen.	It's a book. It isn't a notebook.	**Conversation:** How are you? I'm fine. Thank you.	Is it a circle? Yes, it is. No, it isn't.
		Be friendly.	

Unit 2 Art Class

Lesson 1	Lesson 2	Lesson 3	Lesson 4
Art Supplies: paint, paper, chalk, yarn, glue, tape	**Colors:** red, yellow, blue, white, black	**Story: The Blue Paint**	**Colors:** green, purple, orange, pink, gray, brown
This is paint. What's this? This is paint.	What color is it? It's red.	**Conversation:** Let's share. OK.	Blue and yellow make green.
		Be nice.	

Review 1   Units 1 and 2   **Phonics**   **b**ag, **b**ug, **p**op, **p**it, **t**ag, **t**op, **d**ad, **d**ig, **m**at, **m**ud, **n**ap, **n**od

Unit 3 Birthday Party

Lesson 1	Lesson 2	Lesson 3	Lesson 4
Numbers: one, two, three, four, five, six, seven, eight, nine, ten, eleven, twelve	**Toys:** doll, dolls, ball, balls, car, cars, kite, kites	**Story: My Turn!**	**Toys:** game, marble, puzzle, card
I'm seven. How old are you? I'm eight.	How many dolls? One doll. Two dolls.	**Conversation:** It's your turn. Thank you.	I have one game. I have two games.
		Be fair.	

Unit 4 Home

Lesson 1	Lesson 2	Lesson 3	Lesson 4
Family: mother, father, brother, sister, grandmother, grandfather	**Food:** juice, chicken, fish, ice cream	**Story: Cookies**	**Food:** pizza, rice, cake, bread
This is my mother. Who's this? This is my mother.	I like juice. I don't like juice.	**Conversation:** Here you are. Thank you. You're welcome.	What's this? This is pizza. I like pizza.
		Be kind.	

Review 2   Units 3 and 4   **Phonics**   **b**at, **m**ap, b**e**d, n**e**t, p**i**n, b**i**b, **m**op, **p**ot, t**u**b, n**u**t

Unit 5 **The Park**

Lesson 1	Lesson 2	Lesson 3	Lesson 4
Nature: flower, tree, rock, river, hill, lake	**Playtime:** play soccer, jump rope, fly a kite, ride a bike	**Story: My Kite!**	**Animals:** turtle, frog, spider, ant
I can see a flower.	I can play soccer.	**Conversation:**	Can you see a turtle?
I can see flowers.	I can't play soccer.	Please help me.	Can you see an ant?
What can you see?		Sure.	Yes, I can.
I can see a flower.			No, I can't.
I can see flowers.		Be helpful.	

Unit 6 **The Zoo**

Lesson 1	Lesson 2	Lesson 3	Lesson 4
Animals: monkey, elephant, tiger, bear, kangaroo, penguin	**Animals:** snake, giraffe, lion, zebra	**Story: Where's Danny?**	**Abilities:** run, hop, swim, walk
The monkey is in the tree.	Where are the snakes?	**Conversation**	Can zebras run?
Where is the monkey?	They're on the rock.	I'm sorry.	Yes, they can.
It's on the rock.		That's OK.	No, they can't.
		Be safe.	

Review 3 Units 5 and 6   **Phonics** fan, fox, van, vet, six, sun, zap, zip, red, rug, log, lip

Unit 7 **Science Day**

Lesson 1	Lesson 2	Lesson 3	Lesson 4
My Body: arm, hand, finger, leg, foot, toe	**My Face:** eye, nose, mouth, ear	**Story: I Can't See!**	**Healthy Habits:** wash my face, wash my hands, brush my hair, brush my teeth
What's this?	Is this my eye?	**Conversation:**	
This is my arm.	Yes, it is.	Excuse me.	I can wash my face.
What are these?	No, it isn't.	Sure.	
These are my arms.	Are these my eyes?	Thank you.	
	Yes, they are.		
	No, they aren't.	Be polite.	

Unit 8 **The Toy Store**

Lesson 1	Lesson 2	Lesson 3	Lesson 4
Adjectives: old, new, big, small, long, short	**Adjectives:** fast, slow, noisy, quiet	**Story: Please Be Quiet**	**Transportation:** bus, truck, train, boat
That's an old bike.	Is that a fast car?	**Conversation:**	What's this?
Those are new bikes.	Yes, it is.	Please be quiet.	What's that?
What's that?	No, it isn't.	OK. I'm sorry.	It's an old bus.
That's an old doll.	Are those fast cars?	Thanks.	What are these?
What are those?	Yes, they are.		What are those?
Those are new bikes.	No, they aren't.	Be nice.	They're new buses.

Review 4 Units 7 and 8   **Phonics** rake, vase, beet, peek, dive, lime, rose, bone, mule, cube

Word List